Thank You, Lord

A Collection of Poems

Written and Illustrated by
Gladys Church Mayes

Gratefully Yours,

Gladys

DEDICATION

To all the Angels who have touched my life.

Thank You, Lord
Gladys Church Mayes
© 2013 ALL RIGHTS RESERVED.

ISBN: 978-0-9892582-0-3

Table Of Contents

In Remembrance Of Him	9
Passing On The Blessing	10
A Feeling of Love	11
The Banquet Table	12
My Hungry Soul	13
Christ In Your Heart	15
Beauty of God's Work	16
Practice Makes Perfect	17
The Fountain of Living Water	19
Just Inside The Golden Gate	20
God's Measure	21
Golden Apples	23
Suffer Little Children	24
As A Child	25
Walking The Hills With Jesus	27
A Safe Place To Cry	28
We're All The Same	29
Salt Of The Earth	31
My Savior And My Friend	32
Sunshine In My Soul	33
If I Could	34
The Longer I Know Him	35
In Heaven's Court	36
Dear Jesus, Touch Me	37
When I See My Savior's Face	38
A Walk In The Woods	39
I'm Falling In Love	40
Not Guilty	41
The Valley Will Bloom Again	43
What Did You Do Today	44
Angel Wings	45

One Drop Of Water	46
Building A Cathedral	47
Singing In The Right Key	48
The Final Healing	49
The Great Potter's Wheel	51
The Many Names Of Jesus	52
Merry Christmas Forever	53
Love I Had Never Known	54
The Mark Of God's Blessing	55
Rain On The Desert	57
A Golden Crown	58
I Trust God	59
Give Us Grace To Love You More	60
Out Of The Ashes	61
My Roots	62
My Secret Partner	63
The Value Of The Heart	64
Anytime, Any Place	65
Happy Is The Man	66
My Eyes Are On Jesus	67
What Would Jesus Say	68
Thank You, Lord	69

INTRODUCTION

At the end of a very long journey, how do we measure its success. From a childhood spent in foster homes to being a lonely old recluse............seems it's back where I started for the world has passed me by.

Still many years ago I was blessed to find my way to Jesus. Like the woman at the well, the Lord filled my cup with living water - God's mercy and loving grace.

The true meaning of creative prayer is that we don't have to limit our prayers to words alone. We can communicate with our creator with the language of the heart through words, music and art.

Through all the good and bad, using my God given talents, I managed to live a productive life.

Gladys C. Mayes

In Remembrance of Him

The night of His betrayal they gathered around,
Celebrating the Passover with bread and wine.
At the table with Jesus the disciples gave thanks,
Was the last meal together with their Savior divine.

Christ said, "Eat, this is my body," breaking the bread,
Then gave it His blessing as He served one by one.
"And this wine is my blood that will be shed on the cross,"
Christ Jesus came to give His life as God's only Son.

In remembrance of Him, of His great sacrifice,
In remembrance of Him, crucified for our sin.
With bread and the wine we share communion in grace,
This we do, with gratitude, in remembrance of Him.

Gladys C. Mayes

Passing On The Blessing

A loved one brought me flowers much to my delight,
With a mixture of colors, what a beautiful sight.
So I painted them on canvas to capture for all time,
To always remember the blessing she made mine.

When the picture was finished I still felt incomplete,
So I carried the flowers to someone down the street.
Sick and lonely, it brightened up their day,
We can pass on the blessing in so many ways.

Passing on the blessing, the love of God to share,
Passing on the blessing, our faith we can declare.
Sharing such love, we all can do our part,
Passing on the blessing, a gift from heart to heart.

Gladys C. Mayes

A Feeling Of Love

Many years ago I walked the aisle,
In a little church beneath the pines.
But in my youth soon drifted away,
Seeking that fortune I believed was mine.

Then traveled for years from place to place,
Entered cathedrals reaching the sky.
Met many people both rich and poor,
Still in a crowd so lonely was I.

When I returned seemed nothing had changed,
In that little church beneath the pines,
The music sweet, voices ringing clear,
Praising the Savior through endless time.

A feeling of love was what I longed for,
What we all want and need is love.
God in heaven looks down on us all ,
In His family there's a feeling of love.

Gladys C. Mayes

The Banquet Table

Everyone is welcome with a warm embrace,
At the Master's table, He longs to see your face.
You may come in satin or old filthy rags,
He cares not for the outside nor coins in money bags.

Why are you waiting, they are pouring up the wine,
At the banquet table with our Savior divine.
You were sin laden, now you have been atoned,
Once you feed at His table, your soul is His alone.

Someone really loves you, there's no need to hide,
All through eternity His great love will abide.
Hurry to the table, you must be in place,
For now your soul has been saved by His kind loving grace.

The banquet table is ready, you don't have to bring one thing,
For heaven's banquet table is set to please the King.
There's an abundance of love on God's menu,
At the banquet table, they have set a place for you.

Gladys C. Mayes

My Hungry Soul

My soul was so hungry for comfort from the Lord,
It had been shattered by life's cruel wicked sword.
So I searched to find Him for heaven was my goal,
He'd wash my sins away and feed my hungry soul.

This is where I found Him, was on my knees one night,
He heard my feeble pleading made my life turn bright.
I'll always be thankful for His great wondrous love,
He will feed my soul 'til I reach my home above.

Life can be so dreary when you travel alone,
The pathway is narrow, so dark and full of stone.
Take the hand of Jesus, He'll help you on your way,
He will give you hope and comfort to face every day.

My hungry soul is satisfied with daily bread,
The hungry souls of all His sheep will all be fed.
My hungry soul, my spirit knows He will console,
With love sublime my Jesus feeds my hungry soul.

Gladys C. Mayes

Christ In Your Heart

Don't let others spoil your faith with their philosophy,
Don't let them take away the joy in your heart.
Don't ever doubt for even one tragic moment,
That Christ is Lord and from Him never depart.

If you're searching in this world and all you do is fail,
To find the Christian way, your heart to renew.
Remember Christ, Who said, know Me, know My doctrine,
Give Him your heart and to Him always be true.

When the time comes and your heart is right, your mind will follow,
For in your heart Christ will give you a sweet new song.
And there will be no more fear of things yet to come,
Just hold on to His love and your faith will grow strong.

Christ in your heart is your only hope of glory,
Without His love and mercy, we'd be a wasted loss.
Christ in your heart means love in your life,
He'll fill your heart when you kneel at the foot of the cross.

Gladys C. Mayes

Beauty Of God's Work

If as the artist with a brush I could share,
And capture the beauty of God's work that's everywhere.
At the top of the canvas I'd start with the sky,
With colorful rainbows and clouds drifting by.
Then the mountains so high of purple tone hue,
Green valleys, dark shadows and peaks shining through.
But soon I'd be overwhelmed, where would I begin,
For this pair of eyes couldn't take it all in.

If as the poet I could find words in the pen,
Write about God's love with praise, hallelujah, amen.
How He made all the planets in the universe so grand,
Such beautiful creatures and then He made man.
Christ is born, suffered and died to rise the third day,
His precious blood was shed to wash our sins away.
All these things were written long before my time,
My words could not improve the beauty or rhyme.

Oh the beauty of God's work, man must proclaim,
Since beginning of time he has tried to explain.
But the greatness of such beauty he can't comprehend,
It can never be captured by mere mortal men.

Gladys C. Mayes

Practice Makes Perfect

Let us practice loving each other everyday,
God gives the power so open up your heart.
The Holy Spirit fills it with love we can share,
God knows we're not perfect and all have missed his mark.

Let us practice doing good deeds for everyone,
And feel the freedom of God's great loving grace.
At times if we're rejected and misunderstood,
Wish them well and bless them to stay in God's embrace.

It takes practice learning the meaning of God's love,
Forgiving ourselves, we all have sad regrets.
But just to know God loves us helps us carry on,
We can cling to His love that forgives and forgets.

Practice makes perfect, it's the way to victory,
Put into practice God's love we all receive.
Practice makes perfect, it's our mission for life,
Practice makes perfect, in God's children that believe.

Gladys C. Mayes

The Fountain Of Living Water

There's an unquenching thirst nothing can satisfy,
When your heart has been broken, your soul is parched and dry.
But there's a place of refreshment with water crystal clear,
The lamb of God will lead you, all thirst will disappear.

The water flows freely from the great throne of God,
That was hewed from the living rock by His most Holy rod.
The fountain of life is Jesus, whose light will show the way,
It's where every thirsty soul can be fulfilled today.

It's the fountain of living water, an endless supply,
That sparkles in the sunlight that soars up to the sky.
Come drink from this fountain, your faith it will restore,
The fountain of living water that flows forevermore.

Gladys C. Mayes

Just Inside The Golden Gate

I deserve no special place in my Father's great estate,
For often times I fall in a sad and sinful state.
But by His loving grace there will be a place for me,
Where I will find peace at last, my spirit to be free.

When I step inside the gate, I will be no stranger there,
I may be dressed in rags, it won't matter what I wear.
The keeper of the gate will point out my every turn,
For someone has paid my way, something I could not earn.

As I step inside the gate, this old body will be whole,
My voice will shout His praise with a happy thankful soul,
I'll hear the angels sing, I'll drink from the crystal sea,
With my Heavenly Father for all eternity.

Just inside the golden gate, I will enter one day,
At my appointed time, I'm traveling on my way.
Just inside the golden gate, there I'll patiently wait,
For a glimpse of my Jesus, just inside the golden gate.

Gladys C. Mayes

God's Measure

The family circle broken, joy and hope was gone,
So I grew up with strangers, where I never belonged.
They taught their religions and never spared the rod,
But even down on my knees, I wondered, where was God.

To earn their love I worked hard, wanting so much to please,
But seeing me through their eyes made me more ill at ease.
Then God sent true love, someone to share this life,
And then for good measure, the strength to grow and thrive.

The world has passed me by now, it's moving so fast,
And soon I'll be going home and loving arms at last.
For God knows my journey, My struggles from the start,
He put beauty in my soul and music in my heart.

God's measure is with mercy on scales just and fair.
Above and beyond man's measure, no court room could compare.
The Son of God, Christ Jesus was sent to show the way,
So trust in God's measure and forgiveness every day.

Gladys C. Mayes

Golden Apples

Like precious gold God's love shines forever,
Like the harvest of joy that's yet to come.
We gather together with our baskets,
Knowing there is enough for everyone.

Hope of the heart is our silver lining,
With redemption a promise we can hold.
Just one mustard seed with faith and courage,
Can be as fruitful as a thousand fold.

God gives us all such wonderful blessings,
From His storehouse so rich with many gifts.
The love of Jesus is always with us,
To forgive and our spirits to uplift.

Golden apples in a silver basket,
Filled with blessings that never depart.
Golden apples in a silver basket,
Fruits of the spirit fills our empty hearts

Gladys C. Mayes

Suffer The Little Children

If Christ came back to earth today and found this world of woe,
With drought and famine everywhere and wars that take its toll.
Sadly lost in the trouble and pain, the little children pay,
If Christ should tell us what to do, we know what He would say.

Let us help the little children that live around this earth,
We cannot let them waste away, we know what they are worth.
So many need fresh water and a big piece of bread,
Let us share with them our blessings until they all are fed.

In this great land of plenty, childhood should be a joy,
But in the mist of this bounty, they're tossed about like toys.
If our children are neglected and their home life a wreck,
Christ said, It's better to have a rock tied around your neck.

Suffer the little children to come unto Me,
I'll take them up in My arms, fill all their hearts with glee.
Do for the least one, oh please listen to My call,
Suffer the little children for I bless one and all.

Gladys C. Mayes

As A Child

As a child I heard someone singing,
About a love so sweet and new.
I asked, who could love them,
With a love so precious and true.
That's when I heard about Jesus,
How God sent Him to earth as a babe.
The man who died at Calvary,
For a sinner like me to save.

Like a child I still go to Jesus,
When all my strength and hope is gone.
I know He will hear me,
For His voice comes to me so strong.
Take up your cross, do not worry,
You will know all the answers someday.
Until then He will walk with me,
And from Him I will never stray.

As a child of God, I have a Savior
Who walks and talks with me each day.
Like a child I trust Him completely,
Meek and mild as a child all the way.

Gladys C. Mayes

Walking The Hills With Jesus

Walking the hills with Jesus, climbing the mountains steep,
Traveling the lonesome valley, crossing waters running deep.
I've walked along the sea shore, seen sunsets beyond compare,
I may have seemed all alone, but my Jesus Christ was there.

Passing thru darkest shadows, I walk and will not faint,
My body weak and weary, still I have not one complaint.
For I know who walks with me, in faith I can walk upright,
And each step along the way, I'm walking in His light.

Jesus walks beside me every hour of the day,
For without His tender mercy, I'm just a piece of clay.
My fears are put to rest for His spirit holds my hand,
When I fall to my knees again, He'll help me stand.

I've walked the hills with Jesus, walked with the living Lord,
Each day I walk with Jesus, my heart strikes a happy chord.
I feel His Holy presence and God's love from above,
As I walk the hills with Jesus forever safe in His love.

Gladys C. Mayes

A Safe Place To Cry

Hold your head up high, put on a happy face,
Step out in the world to earn that special place.
Then stumble and fall, for hard as you try,
You will need a refuge, a safe place to cry.

Perhaps the shoulder of a dear faithful friend,
In the arms of love, someone there to the end.
A safe place to cry when no one seems to care,
Go into your closet and find Jesus there.

A safe place to cry can wash your fears away,
Help find the courage to face another day.
Smiling thru the tears beneath a stormy sky.
Yes, God will provide you a safe place to cry.

Gladys C. Mayes

We're All The Same

No matter our birth place or the color of our skin,
We are all God's children, so we're next of kin.
Like a beautiful rainbow that makes a perfect blend,
We are on this earth together so why can't we be friends?

We share the same emotions, we love, we laugh and cry,
And hope lives in our hearts 'til the day we die.
For inside we're just the same, no matter race or creed,
And to be loved will always be every human's need.

So let us all celebrate, give thanks to God above,
Sing our hymns together with hearts filled with love.
Let us share God's great blessings, His wonders to behold,
Then we will walk together on streets that are paved with gold.

We're all the same in God's eyes, He sees inside the heart,
For He's the great creator, we're each His work of art.
We're all the same and in His name, His love is there to claim,
For love sees no color and God says we're all the same.

Gladys C. Mayes

Salt Of The Earth

How we work and slave to get to the top,
Just to call ourselves the cream of the crop.
Then we say we'll do what God leads us to,
But still we ask what that dollar will do.

We judge a man by the clothes on his back,
Is his house on the wrong side of the tracks.
We count his worth by the things that he owns,
One look in his heart, his values are known.

The salt of the earth is what we could be,
Down to earth and humble, love given free.
The pride in our wealth must be set aside,
And the blessings received let us divide.

Jesus called His disciples, the salt of the earth,
The salt of the earth share a great rebirth.
And in a world of greed they stand apart,
The salt of the earth have love in their hearts.

Gladys C. Mayes

My Savior My Friend

There's someone in my life who never lets me down,
He's the very best friend that I have ever found.
He's always there with me every night and day,
And when troubles come around all I have to do is pray.

Let me tell you more about my Savior and my friend,
He died for you and me to wash away our sin.
He knows all about us and loves us all the same,
His love is there for everyone to claim.

Jesus Christ the living Lord is knocking at your door,
Waiting to share His love with you forevermore.
So open up your heart and let Him set you free
His love is everlasting through eternity.

Let me introduce you to my Savior and my Friend,
He's the friend I always like to recommend.
All you have to say is, please Jesus, take my hand,
So come and meet my Savior and my Friend.

Gladys C. Mayes

Sunshine In My Soul

There is such a glow, everywhere I go,
Though the skies turn gray, there's one thing I know.
God is always near, He is in control,
There's no time for crying with sunshine in my soul.

The days of my life may get dark as night,
But He'll make a path as a shining light.
And His love for me never will decline,
I am filled with His love and I'll let my little light so shine.

There's a piece of heaven right here on this earth,
With the love of Jesus, faith will have rebirth.
So when I get lonely, my heart He will console,
And replace my sadness with sunshine in my soul.

There's sunshine in my soul and my spirits fly,
I can't see a single cloud in the sky.
My mind and my soul has a special goal,
I'll always be happy with sunshine in my soul.

Gladys C. Mayes

If I Could

If I could anoint my Lord and bathe His feet,
And gently dry them with my hair.
I'd draw fresh water from the well,
And with perfume sweeten the air.
If my Lord were to sit at my table,
Oh what a grand meal I would prepare.
To know His grace and be so blest,
In His presence my faith to declare.

If I could have followed Him to the cruel cross
When Jesus died at Calvary.
Where tears were falling with His blood,
That He shed there for you and me.
On the third day He's not where they laid Him,
An empty tomb, the stone rolled away.
The angel said, He is not dead,
Christ has risen, Oh glorious day.

If I could compose a hymn of love and praise,
And be a witness to His name.
With the words of truth from Christ the King,
All His miracles to proclaim.
If I could touch an aching heart with my music,
Blest by the angels from up above.
I'd lead the world to sing as one,
In the spirit of God's perfect love.

Oh, if I could, I surely would,
Praise the Lord forever more.

Gladys Church Mayes

The Longer I Know Him

Once I was fearful, forsaken, alone,
Traveling a dark path, no one to call my own.
Searching and crying for someone to hold,
Then came dear Jesus, I'm now in His fold.

The power of love is a wonderful thing,
And as time goes by, my heart begins to sing.
The longer I know Him, the more I believe,
Day by day His love I gladly receive.

The longer I know Him, my love grows and grows,
The longer He loves me, my heart over flows.
The longer I know Him, forever that will be okay,
The longer I know Him, the Man of Galilee.

Gladys C. Mayes

In Heaven's Court

In Heaven's court the trumpets sound,
In heaven's court where the Lord is King.
The sun and the moon are witnesses,
Where God is judge of everything.

The Holy Spirit fills the halls,
An anthem of praise a band will play.
A choir of a million angels sing,
All God's great glory on display.

Before His throne someday we'll stand,
With our heads bowed low as fears depart.
For His judgment is so just and fair,
And He alone sees in our hearts.

In heaven's court each soul will come,
As prophets of all the tribes report.
In heaven's court all sins resolved,
When all is called to order in heaven's court.

Gladys C. Mayes

Dear Jesus, Touch Me

Jesus has the healing touch, He gave sight to the blind,
He mends the broken hearted, a healer of all mankind.
Jesus made the lame to walk, He set the captive free,
He laid His hands on Lazarus, I need His hands on me.

With the stroke of His great hands, He gives all of His love,
Ever so strong and mighty but soft as a velvet glove.
And He knows my mind, my heart, each and my every need,
Of all my pain and grieving and all of my misdeeds.

When I get His blessed touch, I'll make a brand new start,
He'll take away the hurting that's breaking my poor heart.
So I'm down here on my knees, waiting so patiently,
Soon He will lift me upward, out of this troubled sea.

I need His healing touch, my life needs much repair,
The great physician's touch, I need His tender care.
No one else can save me now, my Savior only Thee,
I need Your healing touch, dear Jesus, touch me.

Gladys C. Mayes

When I See My Savior's Face

It was early in the morning, after a long dreadful night,
The sweet love of my life was losing a hopeless fight.
He'd been searching for hours for something lost in his mind,
When his weariness turned to sleep, he was at peace for a time.

With a heavy heart I crumbled with the breaking of the dawn,
Oh GOD! what can I do? All my strength and hope is gone.
Then a stillness fell over me as my heart skipped a beat,
Someone's in the room wearing a robe and sandals on His feet.

I did not look into His eyes, oh how dare I be so bold,
Though not a word was spoken, still my heart felt consoled.
Lost in the moment, it's hard to say how long He stayed,
But I know He was near me through all those sad and troubled days.

Now my loved one is with Jesus and he's waiting for me there,
So in my loneliness, I hold to the love we shared.
Since that day my faith has grown in God's loving grace,
And when I get to heaven, I'll finally see my Savior's face.

Gladys C. Mayes

A Walk In The Woods

Is your life filled with trouble, are you misunderstood,
And you keep on saying, you'd change if you could.
You can't explain your feelings, a bad attitude,
You can find peace of mind if you find solitude.

Just lay down your tired body 'neath an old oak tree,
Then count all your blessings, your good fortune you will see.
The blue sky above you, the good earth 'neath your head,
It's a promise of tomorrow, you'll never be misled.

When Jesus was tired and troubled, He would take a walk,
To a quiet little garden, to His Father He would talk.
There He would bow down on bended knee,
So follow in His footsteps and your soul will be set free.

A walk in the woods all alone with the Lord,
A little talk with Jesus when life gets too hard.
Put your life in His hands, it will do so much good,
Just you, God and nature, a walk in the woods.

Gladys C. Mayes

I'm Falling In Love With Jesus

There's a feeling coming over me, I've never had before,
Something deep in my heart that will last forevermore.
A love not found on earth, not in this human race,
Of praise and adoration for a much higher place.

Many years I've been searching for, a love to fill my heart.
In that dark and empty place where it had been torn apart.
I found a wondrous love with such a healing touch,
Now I'm very happy that I love Him so much.

Before Jesus came into my life, I had no hope at all,
With my fears hid away behind a tall barren wall.
In need of true love, one that I could return,
The meaning of loving was a lesson hard to learn.

Oh I'm falling in love with Jesus, falling in love with the Lord.
Falling in love with Jesus, singing a happy chord.
I know too that He loves me, my Savior and dearest friend,
I'm falling in love with Jesus, a love that will never end.

Gladys C. Mayes

Not Guilty

Guilty was the verdict though His heart was pure as gold,
When Jesus stood before the court, that's the story we've been told.
They nailed Him to the cross to die at Calvary,
He gave His life to save us, poor sinners like you and me.

We'll enter God's courtroom one by one on judgment day,
Everyone begging for mercy for we fail in many ways.
We're all so unworthy to enter heaven's gate,
Hell would be our destiny, Jesus saved us from that fate.

Not guilty, not guilty, the angels will proclaim,
Not guilty, not guilty, Jesus suffered all our shame.
Because of His love, we'll find a resting place,
Not guilty, not guilty, we'll receive His saving grace.

Gladys C. Mayes

The Valley Will Bloom Again

The cold winds of sorrow will come,
And tears of pain, like rain will flow.
The sun will hide behind a dreary sky,
All will be still in the valley below.

But once the storm has blown over,
All our fears will be washed away.
Birds will sing again, flowers burst into bloom,
The valley will be beautiful on that day.

Passing through the valley of death,
The good Shepherd will take our hand,
He will lead us down that long dark path,
To a beautiful heavenly land.

The valley will bloom again, a promise true,
Every heart will be filled with love that never ends.
When Jesus Christ returns to rule the universe,
On that beautiful day, the valley will bloom again.

Gladys C. Mayes

What Did You Do Today

What did you do today for Jesus,
Just one golden deed to attain.
Did you speak kind to that stranger,
And with someone share in their pain.

Did you give thanks for all your blessings,
That God has showered on you.
Did you say grace at your table,
And ask God your faith to renew.

Did you remember The Lord Jesus,
How He died to set our souls free.
All the blessings we have received,
We owe to the man of Galilee.

What did you do today for that beggar,
To help fill his hunger without delay.
What did you do for Jesus,
Oh what did you do today.

Gladys C. Mayes

Angel Wings

Feel the breeze on your skin, that's the touch of angel wings,
For the mystery of God is a wondrous thing.
Like the answer to a prayer made by someone who cares,
Or the warmth of an embrace when it's love we share.

My life has been blest with such compassion everyday,
For my guardian angel helps me on my way.
Perhaps I may seem lost but they'll find me anywhere,
In the shadow of angel wings there's shelter there.

In the sweet by and by, I'll fly up through the sky,
On angel wings I'll tell this world good-bye.
When I reach the golden gate as all the heavens sing,
In a robe of white I'll receive my angel wings.

Gladys C. Mayes

One Drop Of Water

One by one, drop by drop, from up above,
A sign of God's favor cleansing souls with love.
Raindrops from heaven, how softly they fall,
That's God's salvation touching one and all.

Drink it up, every drop, take time to pray,
With bread and the water, give thanks all your days.
Sure as the ocean will flow with the tide,
All God's creations will be satisfied.

Drop by drop on the cross to set man free,
Christ Jesus shed His blood, died at Calvary.
With God's forgiveness, His mercy attained,
The peace that we'll find, forever remains.

One drop of water, our strength to regain,
Drink the living water, never thirst again.
With droplets of blessings, our faith will survive,
One drop of water, gives everlasting life.

Gladys C. Mayes

Building A Cathedral

Moses built the first tabernacle,
For his people wandering in the wilderness.
Considered a place of the presence of God,
Forever blest by His Holiness.

King Solomon built a great temple,
With precious treasures of silver and gold.
An altar was built for the blood sacrifice,
Offerings for sin that all could behold.

Today men still build great cathedrals,
As they worship God, all power up on high.
Every heart can be a sanctuary of God,
Filled with love that always satisfies.

I've been building a cathedral seen only in my mind,
The steeple my arms reaching upward to the sky.
The organ music, the love sung in my heart.
Stained glass windows, God's creations, reflected in my eyes.

Gladys C. Mayes

Singing In The Right Key

Singing is a blessing from above,
A gift of the angels wrapped in heavenly love.
For music brings joy to the human heart,
Each soul a melody, love to impart.

We must keep on singing day by day,
In all kinds of weather, each step of the way.
But no matter our troubles, we can agree,
To sing about Jesus is the right key.

Sing another encore loud and clear,
In the key of Jesus with love and good cheer.
So let us have a happy attitude,
And every heart be filled with gratitude.

Singing in the right key, faithful evermore,
Singing in the right key, opens heaven's door.
Singing of God's mercy that sets us free,
Singing in the right key, our praise Lord to Thee.

Gladys C. Mayes

The Final Healing

No more pain my friend for it's all over,
I'll say good bye as you go on your way.
No more grief for your troubles have ended,
God healed your body and your soul today.

All through life we ask God for His mercy,
When we are broken we pray to be made whole.
Time after time God comes to restore us,
To heal the sick and mend the inner soul.

But all things come to a final chapter,
Though we fall short, God hears our last request.
The path of life has a lonely passage,
Where God fills wounded hearts with peace and rest.

The final healing has a wonderful purpose,
It opens the gate to that heavenly place.
The final healer receives us as His angels,
To live forever in God's great love and grace.

Gladys C. Mayes

The Great Potter's Wheel

The old potter keeps on turning the wheel,
To work clay and water with his skillful hands.
Shaping and sanding to cast into the fire,
For all of his vessels are in great demand.

God is the potter who's shaping my life,
I'm spinning and changing each passing day.
Trials mixed with blessing like the sun with the rain,
And God is still shaping this old piece of clay.

God created man from dust of the earth,
He threw in the heavens each bright shining star.
Jesus placed clay on the eyes of the blind,
God gave Him the power to heal every scar.

On the great potter's wheel I patiently wait,
Knowing the beauty of God's earthenware.
I trust in His mercy as I yield to His will,
On the great potter's wheel, I am safe in His care.

Gladys C. Mayes

The Many Names Of Jesus

To God the Father, Jesus is His only Son,
The brightness of God's glory, the Anointed One.
Light of the world forever, no beginning or end,
He's the blessed Savior and to heaven did ascend.

To all the nations, He's the teacher of God's word,
King of the Jews, the Messiah and the Lord of lords.
He lived His life for others, the Man of Galilee,
Then the cross He carried, crucified at Calvary.

To me a sinner drifting on the sea of life,
Today He is my Shepherd through trouble and strife.
He's the blessed Redeemer, who saves our sin sick soul,
We thank God for Jesus, whose healing touch makes us whole.

The many names of Jesus, spoken in many tongues,
With words put to music, His praise forever sung.
The bread of life for all men, our manna from above,
The many names of Jesus, all have the meaning of love.

Gladys C. Mayes

Merry Christmas Forever

Does Christmas end too soon and then forgotten,
Just like the Christmas tree and pretty ribbon,
Soon to be cast away, just a memory,
It could never end as we praise God's only Son.

Christmas is a day of great celebration,
And we fill our homes with glitter and bright lights.
It brings us together beneath a shining star,
Just like the shepherds on that first Christmas night.

We adore baby Jesus wrapped in swaddling cloth,
As our Christmas carols softly fill the air.
A day of remembrance with hearts blessed with giving,
Our gift to You dear Jesus is the love that we share.

Merry Christmas forever, Merry Christmas to you,
Don't put Christmas away, God's gift we must treasure.
Keep it safe in your heart all of your days,
Merry Christmas to you, Merry Christmas forever.

Gladys C. Mayes

Love I Had Never Known

Do you know how it feels to be alone,
Without family and home to keep you warm.
A lump in your throat, no hope in your heart,
And like me, wondered why you had been born.

For a time it was so hard to believe,
I was safe and that someone did love me.
Soon my doubts were gone, Jesus was the One,
And His love was real, given to me free.

Now I thank you my dear Savior and Lord,
For your patience and everlasting love.
You never gave up, You held out the cup,
I drank my fill of manna from above,

Yes, I found love I had never known,
A love that would never let me down.
The Savior took me in, I found peace within,
Yes, I found love I had never known.

Gladys C. Mayes

The Mark Of God's Blessing

To find an answer is like putting this river in a box,
The waters rushing by as I stand here on this rock.
The current runs too deep and the river is so wide,
That bridge I just crossed over washed away with the tide.

So now I'm watching the wreckage slowly drift away from shore,
To see the death of dreams, how it hurts me to the core.
Seems I have reached the end for the future looks so dark,
But I've been blest with God's love and it has left its mark.

Oh Yes, I have the mark of Jesus on me,
I wear it so proudly for all to see.
The mark of that blessing sets me apart,
With tears in my eyes, there's still hope in my heart.

The mark of God's blessing is heaven's design,
The mark of God has a visible sign.
No matter what happens we can make a new start,
The mark of God's blessing, we wear on our hearts.

Gladys C. Mayes

Rain On The Desert

Are you crossing a desert in dark solitude,
Do you wander about in a somber mood.
Do you stand and watch the restless drifting sand,
Are you lost in a lonely barren land.

Is your heart cold and lifeless, sweet peace can't be found,
Have you lost hope finding green fertile ground.
Searching for a refuge; weary to the bone.
But do not faint for God is still on His throne.

Lost in a desert storm, there's nothing you can see,
And to the high cool mountains you want to flee.
To know the dry desert will return from the dead,
Just to see a rainbow circled overhead.

Like rain on the desert, the Lord gives new life,
Rain on the desert helps nature to survive,
With God's tender mercy, life is made anew,
Like rain on the desert, He gives life to you.

Gladys C. Mayes

A Golden Crown

The emblem of royalty is a golden crown,
But Jesus Christ wore no crown or diamond rings.
He owned no ivory palace, no golden throne,
Even though Jesus was the King of all kings.

The rain of sorrow and pain fell down all around,
This Holy Man, even His life would be His loss.
And the only crown that ever touched His head,
Was a crown of thorns that He wore to the cross.

Jesus gave the world a reason to hope,
Prisoners behind bars found invisible wings.
There were so many souls that came to believe,
That even without a crown, He was the King.

Now for eternity Jesus wears a golden crown,
In heaven He was adorned in all His glory.
He sits on a golden throne with angels at His feet,
A golden crown for the Lord was our victory.

Gladys C. Mayes

I Trust God

My destiny I can't foresee,
But I know my Lord will hear my plea.
He gives me hope and I ensure,
For in His hands, my life's secure.

The question comes, why was I born,
Sometimes I feel so tired and worn.
But patiently I wait to see,
His plans I'll follow faithfully.

I've been blest by His loving grace,
He gives me strength in each trial I face.
To be a Christian I take pride,
Knowing He's always by my side.

I trust God and what's yet to be,
I trust Jesus, He died for you and me.
I trust His love that sets us free,
I trust God for all eternity.

Gladys C. Mayes

Give Us Grace To Love You More

You gave us sight to see your great beauty,
And a voice to use to sing your praise.
Gave the gift of sound to hear for teaching,
To help us on the way for all our days.

You gave the world a bright glimpse of glory,
That gives peace of mind to every soul.
You gave mankind hope for life eternal,
And the weak and suffering You will console.

You gave all for love that's everlasting,
You gave the sweet fresh air that we breathe,
The greatest gift anyone could receive.

By Your loving grace You saved us,
Please Lord give us grace to love You more.
Oh dear Jesus, our Lord and Savior,
Please give us grace to love You more.

Gladys C. Mayes

Out Of The Ashes

In every lifetime there's trouble and pain,
In everyone's life comes sunshine and rain.
Someday your dreams may tumble down,
But out of the ruin, hope can be found.

Out of the ocean of tears that may flow,
You'll find an island and peace for your soul.
There you'll find healing all pain will be gone,
With Jesus beside you rejoice and move on.

Ashes of roses still give off perfume,
Their sweet fragrance can fill every room.
Though we may walk through ashes and dust,
God's love is still there waiting for us.

Out of the ashes spirits will rise,
Out of the ashes we can survive.
Out of the darkness and fear in the night,
Out of the ashes and into God's light.

Gladys C. Mayes

My Roots

No roots, no home place where I can return,
No folks, good memories but still the heart can yearn.
No safe refuge, no peaceful resting place,
Just a wanderlust leaving not a trace,

A house I built one for my earthly stay,
The rooms were filled with treasures that will decay.
I reached for fame, though it was never mine,
But all of these things will be left behind.

My roots though broken have been homeward bound,
I know that someday they'll grow in solid ground.
So on my way I chase away the gloom,
For where God plants me, that's where I must bloom.

Someday I'll be going to a place I call home,
Where the gate will swing wide open, never more to roam.
There my heavenly Father on His throne will welcome me,
My roots I'll plant there beside the crystal sea.

Gladys C. Mayes

My Secret Partner

God is my partner and we're making plans,
He gives the orders, I work with my hands.
He plants the seeds and I harvest the crop,
I'll follow His footsteps to the mountain top.

No need to borrow for His help is free,
For God's in control of my destiny.
I will keep that promise to do my part,
Now my secret partner lives here in my heart.

When I am thirsty, I drink from His cup,
He never fails to lift my spirits up.
God keeps me safe through the darkness of night,
To rise with the sun and then walk in His light.

My secret partner ,my companion for life,
He is my strength through trouble and strife.
My secret partner, on Him I can depend,
He's my secret partner and my best friend.

Gladys C. Mayes

The Values Of The Heart

We all know the value of the dollar,
We want a fair exchange on our return.
So we seek our wealth in gold and silver,
For we're measured by the money we earn.

But the heart of a man is his treasure,
Filled with God's love and yielding to His will.
As we grow in deeper understanding,
All our needs only Jesus can fulfill.

We know Jesus was born in a manger,
To die on the cross by the hands of man.
We want to follow in His footsteps,
Without the strife and His pain if we can.

So why do we Christians shoot our wounded,
Or kick a broken soul when they are down.
That could be Jesus standing in their shoes,
The value of their hearts will win a crown.

The values of the heart are ever changing,
Like a rainbow blending colors in the sky.
The values of the heart forever seeking,
The values of the heart always multiply.

Gladys C. Mayes

Any Time, Any Place

When there's no one to love me and I'm feeling so alone,
When there's no place to be found that really feels like home.
When the world forsakes me, there's still somewhere to go,
There will always be Jesus, God knows I need Him so.

When my heart has been broken and there's no peace of mind,
If I get down on my knees, contentment can be found.
So when deep in sorrow He'll wash away the tears,
For to know of His love, there's nothing to be feared.

So I count all my blessings and give thanks everyday,
And try never to worry of things to come my way.
Now when I get weary and start to lose the fight,
I pray to dear Jesus to help me through the night.

Anytime, any place, I can be with Jesus,
Anytime, any place life can be victorious.
Anytime, any place to receive my Savior's grace,
I can feel His presence, anytime, any place.

Gladys C. Mayes

Happy Is The Man

Man is born unto trouble all of his days,
To labor through sorrow every step of the way.
Helpless and hopeless to what he could be,
Until he meets the Son of God, the Man of Galilee.

Man is cruel without God's love deep in his heart,
He can't live on bread alone, that's just a small part.
Praying to Jesus his life to embrace,
With true faith find redemption, God's mercy and His grace.

Man is blest beyond measure with peace of mind,
There's a happy ending when contentment he finds.
Rich man or poor man, God will fill each soul,
Every need will be fulfilled when God is in control.

Happy is the man who can truly believe,
In the name of Jesus, His blessings to receive.
To trust in the Lord and know he's in God's plan,
Behold through all tribulations, happy is the man.

Gladys C. Mayes

My Eyes Are On Jesus

I started my journey with a need to belong,
Consumed with a hunger growing ever so strong.
My heart in a vacuum on a long hopeless race,
With the illusion I'd find that perfect place.

Like a fool believing I was on the right track,
To realize one day that I'd fallen through the cracks.
There in my solitude I heard my Jesus say,
There is a place for you, I'll show you the way.

My burden has lifted, I accept who I am,
For He's the Shepherd who rescues every lamb.
In spite of my weakness, all my failures and fear,
He'll never leave me, His love is always near.

My eyes are on Jesus for I know without a doubt,
He's on a higher level, on the heavenly route.
With my eyes on Jesus, the bright eternal light,
My eyes are on Jesus and I'm forever in His sight.

Gladys C. Mayes

What Would Jesus Say

When Jesus Christ our Lord and Savior,
Came to earth to do His Father's will.
Teaching men about salvation,
For the scriptures Jesus had to fulfill.

He healed the sick and broken hearted,
Forgave poor sinners who'd gone astray.
Doing good in matchless perfection,
With miracles made from sin and decay.

With great mercy that's everlasting,
He'll help you through the darkest of night.
He said, "Be not afraid, I'm with you,
Just follow Me, I'm the way and the light."

What would Jesus say to give us comfort,
His message would be the same today.
So when we're searching for the right answer,
Just remember, what would Jesus say.

Gladys C. Mayes

Thank You, Lord

LORD, You've watched me on life's journey,
Seen the fear that was so deep.
The searching for a safe refuge,
Did my stupidity make You weep?
It seemed that nothing came easy,
Dark clouds always hid the light.
Many times my eyes were down cast,
When I should have kept You in my sight.
The blessing of love I doubted,
Though You never turned Your face.
Thank You, Dear LORD, for Your patience,
Your wondrous love and saving grace.

Gladys C. Mayes